Collected
Poems

Bernard Levinson

Published in 2020 by Hands-On Books
Cape Town, South Africa

www.modjajibooks.co.za

Cover artwork by Sheila Levinson

Book layout by Andy Thesen

Set in Legacy

ISBN: 978-1-928433-12-5

Dedication

For my wife Sheila, our three amazing daughters
and their totally astounding children.

"Thank you."
Can such a simple innocent phrase
complete such a task?
Does it know
it has to cover
45 years
of astonishing
love.
A raging river
of want and need,
and the endless
endless calm
of knowing you are there
at my side.
What wings can I give you?
What powerful hands?

Contents

BOOK 1

From Breakfast to Madness
(Ravan Press, 1974)

Part 1

Dear Anne

When I go from breakfast to madness
dear Anne
with the clouds clutched tight in my hands
and my frail books
filled with worn-out words—
I tell the nurse
this is a rest home for retired spies
cranky characters
talking back to their chairs.
And we both laugh
to ease my pain
and hide for a moment
the sleep walkers
who pace their mops on the burnished floor.

Charles

I think of Charles
who hanged himself
from the lintel of his door.
On the surface of my mind
a single dry leaf floats.
Now it is a hand calling—
now a rusty raft ...
I listen—
there are no demands
no call for help
only the Autumn wind crying.

Elsie

Elsie talked to God from her flat in Hillbrow.
Perched on the edge of her bath
she discussed the price of bread
and the things the butcher said
when she couldn't decide.

She was always grateful that He found her.
Between the Swop Shop and the coffee bar
one could miss the door—
the metal steps to the fourth floor
and the dark corner
where the refuse drain rumbled and coughed.

The sun falls amongst chimneys
Splinters in a million windows—
Are you there Elsie?
Are you there in the darkness—
in your own secret cave
holding the remains of the day in a shopping bag?
Are you talking to God?

Too Many Words

There are too many words.
Each day I drown in words.
Once I sat with a man
each day for six months
and not a word passed between us.
I've never forgotten
how moved I was
by what he said ...
What I'm trying to say
is that I have a need
now and then
to shake the words out of my hair.
All the stale and used-up words—
the frantic panic words
that jump about my desk—
and the heavy meaningful words
that hang like curtains in the air.
The people who spin words about me
holding me tightly to them—
and the people who fill every corner
with urgent words—
every inch of my room—
closing the space
through which they may fall to nothing.
One word would be enough!
Just one word
that I might hold it in my palm
weigh it
and know it.

Your Small Fist

There's no need for words.
Your small fist
cupped in the palm of my hand—
I insinuate a finger
inside the curled barricade—
and read the temperature
the amount of hurt—
the hold-tight pain of your young life.

I remember once before—
my first call to the township
between the steaming huts
on the lip of a makeshift road
where I swung my black bag
brash as a boy
safe in his Medical School.

The dark girl in labour
was younger than I.
A child bearing a child.
I fumbled in my bag
looking for words
among the shoe-horn shapes,
the trumpets and the string.
In the end she cried
and I held her hand ...

The File

The file said
"eight years old"—
and gave a list
of all the homes she'd lived in.
Orphanages,
places of safety—
homes for little girls
who have no home.
The reports were formal.
Factual.
Nowhere
could I find
the little girl.

She was serious.
She held a doll upside down
and waited ...
"Please sir
do you mind if I love you?"

Group Therapy

We were talking about love
(not daring to use that word)
as they sat about me
in a circle.
The boys and the girls
each with a puppet on one hand.

He said—
"Mine's an old man.
He's so very hungry
and so very much alone."
And she in the softest voice—
"My puppet's ugly.
Everyone hates her."

I searched for words
to form a bridge
between them.

The old man looked at the ugly puppet.
The paper heads nodded gravely
while the group waited.

And I, groping in my word-world
waited for the right words
to set them free.

On an impulse,
he stretched forward
and gently swept her hair
out of her face.

Art Therapy

You are painting your past—
weaving a green lattice
with the fingers of both hands—
"I am thinking of the Eiffel Tower."

And I suddenly remember the time
I walked down from the top
through the criss-cross steel
feeling the fear in my legs
the April wind in my hair
and the afternoon sun
catching triangles of sky
and horizon
and Paris giddy below me.
The ascenseur angles past me
going down—
people pressed to its glass side—
faces watching the landscape
and then me
holding up the trembling column
windswept on the labyrinth of stairs
smiling embarrassed
at the box of faces going down—

I sadden when your green girders
become a forest
and you lead me
into your life's wood.
I am thinking of the Eiffel Tower.

Crucifixion

Your painting burns on my desk.
A crucifixion.
Christ in agony—
I can hear you cry
in the red bursting pain—
in the writhing of arms and legs—
"My God—
why hast thou forsaken me?"

Week after week
I have watched your paintings—
sometimes the torn Christ
pulls free, and falls screaming—
mostly he is caught on the cold-cross
his Christ-mouth crying
and the hot tears running across
the limp body
into the heart of my world.

I am your cross.
It is I who hold you fast
in the torment of this love.
In your paintings
a whirlpool-scream fans out—
"I know you will forsake me!
You
who live only in a couch-world—
you
who are also my Mother and my Father—
you too will forsake me!"

Schizophrenia (1)

She was naked when she danced.
A wild crow sat on her head
shrieking the rhythm.
Her young breasts nodded
while her body took the shape of music.

She was dancing for me.
When she found I had not come
she tore the papers and all the magazines,
she trailed the sheets of the wet ward-bed
and smashed a vase on the heavy door.

I found her weeping
amongst her destruction of me,
the black-raven limp and silent.
She sat on the floor
drying the hot storm of her eyes
with the back of her hand.
"We'll let it sleep,
this restless angry bird."
But it wasn't my voice that she heard.

Schizophrenia (2)

You walk like a long-legged bird
lifting your feet
picking your way through the chaos.
Poor lost flamingo
flying forever in the dark world
of drugs, words and psychiatrist couches.
You remind me of buildings
looking raw in the sudden sunlight—
standing tall and thin
bewildered and alone
blinking in this unaccustomed world—
Poor sick flamingo
how shall I lead you out of this madness?

Schizophrenia (3)

He lay under the washbasin dreaming—
counting waves and secret sevens,
seven stars and seven candles,
seven days and the seven years.

I remember that first morning
when I pulled him out by the folds of his coat—
I listened to the magic of his counting—

Three kings on a long journey
two moons for a dark prince
one sun that cannot rise—

Each morning he was there
huddled in the well of his coat
under the washbasin—

Five fingers on one hand
five hands that cannot reach
five mothers crying.

In the shirt-sleeved heat of the ward's sweat
he was there—

Four birds with torn wings
three trees without roots

and on the iron-cold, cement-cold mornings
he was there,
an awkward bundle between the pipes

Two rivers with no end
one bridge that cannot be crossed.

Schizophrenia (4)

I watch you walking in your dream-walk
up and down the empty square
past the one bare tree—
the hard music of the loudspeakers
falling about you.
Your step is unsteady.
An old sailor pacing
the memory of a flat deck
in the roll and pitch of a chronic ward.

I remember you this way
always walking and alone.
I would put you to sleep
setting the lightning loose in your brain—
and always after
I would find you walking alone.

It was August
when they brought you to my room.
"How are you?" I asked.
You lifted your eyebrows—
and your mouth began the search for words.
How long did we stand there
you and I?
Waiting
while you walked your secret desert
looking for words.

"Smoke," you said. Just like that.
Incongruous and final—
Your eyebrows pumping,
your mouth shaping
and reshaping the other words that never came.
Outside
the tree in your square world
had just turned green.

In Your Darkness

In your darkness
where the sick sleep
curled in their blind beds—
There is a splinter of moon,
a surgeon's needle threading the stars
through the wide window of the ward
winding the day's madness
into a long narrow sleep.
Come my friend
there is no need to stand
at the side of your bed
living still your day's dream
while the moon sews the night
into a small dark fist.
Put the voices away
and let this womb accept you.

To Judy

The burning began
before the final flame.
I've watched you fold
your depression
into the lotus position.

I like to believe—
My poor proud Buddha—
that you struck the match
with a nun-like grace.
I shall try to forget
the way you whimpered.
I shall try to forget
the way your eyes searched my face.

Dagga

For three days now
I've listened to the Messiah
on the way to work.
"Everybody shall be exalted" ...
in Oxford Road.
      "I'm getting smaller and greyer."
      He pinched the mouth
      of his cigarette, and seemed
      to suck the tips of his fingers.
"Unto us a child is born."
      With old hands
      cupping
      the burnt-out butt—
"Unto us a son is given."
      "These sick vibes
      freak me out
      Doc
      I'm getting smaller
      and smaller
      I'm afraid the fire
      will never turn green ..."
For three days now
I've listened
to the Messiah.

Going Home

"So you're going home," I say
holding the conversation
in my left hand.
The metronome of your leg
quickens its beat.

Once before we acted out
a "going home".
I was your mother.
You said my breasts were blind—
my arms too stiff to bend.
We began
with a knock on the door,
and I was there
balancing the sun on the edge of my bed.
The world was round
and April burnt on the trees forever—
But you placed the heavy words
on the hook of my tongue
and we stood ...

I take the conversation firmly
in my right hand.
"So you're going home."

Weskoppies Asleep

Weskoppies asleep.
The green roofs
float in the rising heat.
The old trees
bend to the windows
and listen—
the sick are asleep.
They are dreaming—
their tears flow
into the darkness
over the waiting trees.

On duty
I only hear
the hospital breathing,
the corridors
the wooden stairs
the warm core
of this dark world
breathing.

Somewhere in the valley
trains running northwards
call to each other.
The sound swims through the night
into the quiet
of my room.

I am no longer aware
of the sick
hiding in their lonely beds.
Only inside me
the wide questioning eyes
refuse to close.

Hillbrow

They're building a tower in Hillbrow.
At night
a light burns at the top.
A candle for Hillbrow.
For mourning.
For the young man crying
under the bright lights.
I knocked on the dark glasses.
"I saw my spirit," he said,
not letting me in.
"A small spirit
as long as my arm
dressed in a blue suit
with gold buttons.
It was jumping up and down
in my brain."

Once upon the concrete
where the pedlars push
their secret wares
a boy was crucified
against the changing lights.

Encounter Group

The moment we cease to hold each other,
the moment we break faith with one another
the sea engulfs us and the light goes out.
                                        — James Baldwin

I am standing with my eyes shut. Waiting.
At the head of the hall the voice says—
"Touch your neighbour.
Let your hand discover this other world."
This is the beginning.
I lift my hands and wait.
I hear movement.
I feel the air tentatively, waiting.
I slowly advance.
Suddenly it's there.
My hand finds a shoulder.
There are fingers on my arm.
Somewhere inside me I reach for my kitbag.

It's early morning.
The train has arrived at Park Station.
I reach for my kitbag.
All my possessions
my wardrobe, my library, my valuables,
the odds and ends
that shape all I know as me—
comfortably on my shoulder.
I make my way to the tram stop.
Nothing has changed.
I close my eyes
and breathe in the Johannesburg I remember.
Early morning Johannesburg.
The metallic clang of the heavy tram.
I search my bunny-jacket for tram fare.
I am coming home.

The idea leaves me tight with excitement.
I can think of little else.
We pass buildings I know.
The conductor waits at my side
swaying with the tram.
I want to tell him I am going home.
I finger the kitbag at my side,
and wait.
The tram lurches.
I am going home.
I walk from the tram stop,
marching in my boots.
The houses are barely awake.
I sharpen the pistol-crack of my boot
on the empty street.
I swing my free arm.
I am the 6th Army returning.
The street is empty.
I reach the door and ring the bell.

My mother answers the door—
for a moment we face each other.
"I'm home," I say
not sure if my presence is enough—
"You didn't write …"
"I wasn't sure …"
"You're just in time for breakfast …"

"You can open your eyes,"
the voice says.
"Open your eyes and feel your neighbour."
Let your fingers speak.
Let your hands listen.
Discover this other person.

A young woman is standing before me.
Out of my darkness.
I am surprised at the light
and a little afraid.

My hand is on her shoulder.
Her fingers rest on my arm.
She is wearing the sun about her shoulders
showering tassels of sunlight
across her breasts.
I trace the landscape of her neck
with my eyes.
I am aware of silence.
My fingers are mute and heavy.
Odd,
Sitting at the old breakfast table
my kitbag at my side.
We can't easily be parted.
I feel the handle,
the rough canvas side.
We are all here.
My mother, my father, my brother, my sister,
my kitbag and I.
My father breaks the silence inside me.
"You must have seen a lot of things …"
"Yes, I've seen so many things …"
Should I touch their faces?
There is nothing to say.
We smile
and eat.

I wait for the voice.
I wait for my fingers to move.
To shout. To cry.
Her hand is on my chest.

She has found my agony.
Her fingers slip between my ribs.
I feel her searching my darkness.
I rush to the tips of my fingers
falling into touch.

I am in a group
with five others.
We kneel in a circle holding each other.
We gently rock—
enter a common touch
like children rocking.
I stand and allow myself to fall
knowing they will catch me in their arms,
will pass me from arm to arm
cradled
like a small child.
And like a small child
will lower me
touching my body.

My kitbag
and all I know as me
no longer fits my shoulder.

Part 2

To Stand with Old Men

I want to stand with old men
the Tallit* over my head—
I want to cry
and whisper all the old words.
Yet I know
if I could reach into the darkness
I would cry
for yesterday
and for today—
and for my whole life.

* *Jewish prayer shawl*

Kineret

Lake Kineret
I know you
I watch your firefly-fishermen
move in your darkness
awaking a memory deep in my soul.

Kineret
I remember you
for four thousand years
the fires of your fishermen
burn in my blood,
and the nets
drag their fish
to my own secret shore.

Kineret
only now
when I stand in your silence
I know who I am.

Masada

I want to climb Masada—
not the easy way
like a Roman—
But like a Jew
I want to struggle with the east wall.
It's not enough to arrive—
This must be handled like a woman
slowly, holding back the moment.
I'm afraid
of being unable to lose myself.
I'm afraid
I will never find myself.

Poem

Something you said
made me aware
I have daughters—
While you talked
I was walking with a small boy.
You are bewildered.
How can you know I am flying a kite
with my son.
And when I cry
how can you know
he is drawing me to him
with a secret thread ...
You don't know
that the folds of my Tallit
cover his head.

I Once Dreamt

I once dreamt
I made love to a fat woman.
I was too young
to know what to do.
I swam between her thighs
and rose panting
in the heat of her hills.

I now have words
for the dream—
giving the dream
a Mother shape
and an awkward taste.

Once

Once
to make a point
I swept past my Mother's thunder,
past her anger
and past my fear.
Still
I have the pain
here in my chest
where God tore the rib
to make woman.

You tell me she was crying when you phoned her ...

Crying.
That's all I remember.
In spite of the jokes
and funny stories
I only remember the crying.
My mother cried
for all the children
in the neighbourhood.
She cried for Jews
all over the world.
She also cried for me.
Once in a dream
a burst of birds
left my chest.
I knew the birds
were tears.
Once in a dream
a fisherman dragged his net.
I knew the struggle
was mine.
And I knew
the nets would be filled
with her crying.
Mother—
I am standing at your side.
It is Friday night.
The candles are lit.
You are blessing our home
with tears.
There's no room
inside me
to store this weeping.

Part 3

Magaliesberg

The smell of rain-washed grass
spins me back
to the mountains—
      a rough cleft in the tall rocks,
      a grass clearing—and water.
      A low-pitched tent,
      and the sweet taste
      of the warm wet breath of summer morning.
How odd
that in all the fragrance of my garden
a splinter of scent
the merest edge in the evening air
can hold me rooted to yesterday.

Stones

I like to pick up stones
round stones
in the pocket of my palm
telling me secrets of water—
hard smooth secrets—
the wind-smooth pain of small stones.

If you want to understand trees
and rivers and hills,
you have to weigh a stone shape in your fingers
while you walk.

Meeting

She was undressed first.
He put his shoes together.
Folded his glasses.
Placed his underpants
under the trousers.
Each movement
a silence.
Cold floor—
coarse blanket
chafing the skin.
"Would you like me to begin?"
He smoothed his hair
into place.

There should have been rain
and thunder.
In the dreams
she was aware of lightning
helping her open.
In her dreams
the rivers ran
in the hot rain.
Below them a radio coughed
and they listened
to the news.

A Terrorist is Shot

"A terrorist is shot."
This is the caption under the picture.
A thick-set officer
holding a heavy service revolver.
A young man pinned to a post
blindfolded head strangely askew
and his legs slumped.

This death clutches at my soul.
This cold planned drama
between man and man.
This is the Hunter in the night.
The inevitable—
the final
the no-appeal—
And I am the limp puppet
waiting for the end ...

Déjà vu

      The road winds
past the German school—
past the red brick
of the old hotel.
Tense?
Is it rain
fingering the window
of your car?
      The road winds
to the hospital door—
the long passage
and the dark ward.

Troubled?
Is it pain
holding the muscles
of your back?
　　　The road winds
past the German camp—
The rain bursts inside me—
past the red brick crematorium.
No ...
　　　The road winds
to the open door
and the long tunnel
of Dachau.

October 1971

It's raining in Hillbrow.
A poster weeps in the rain.
Words run to rivers.
The word "Detention"
remains.

America

America—
I remember the brainwashed mornings
of my childhood,
standing before the upright piano,
pledging allegiance
to a barber-pole flag,
my eyes always on the day's milk
stacked under the blackboard.
Thirty years later
with snow falling
on the milk-white morning
of my memory—
        I take off the socks
        I wear as gloves,
my-country-tis-of-thee
        I set my odd-shoe foot
        behind the leg of the desk
of-thee-I-sing—
        watching the day's milk
I can never afford—
Land where my father
was always an old man
carrying the Depression home
in his empty hands.
America—
I am surprised
how these old wounds bleed.

Part 4

On Viewing His Paintings

(For Taffy Whippman)

I'm afraid to walk in your pictures.
There's not a scene
I don't know
or have not known
all my life.
I'm not fooled
by the draining of colour
that I might believe
this is only a dream—
I recognise shadows
when only the light is shown.

I'm afraid to walk in your pictures.
Your loneliness
is too much like my own.

To Louie

Why is it I can never think
of those who come here,
suffer a little, and go home?
There must be many who come and go,
feeling easier, pleased to be mended.
I only think of the dead.
The long black cars
waiting unobtrusively.
I think of Mr Momson
in his cold-storage house
stacking bodies on neat tin trays,
and the students perched
on their tombstone benches
irreverently chanting
"Give us this day our daily dead ..."

I walk in your corridor
a little afraid I will find
at some turning
that sinister trolley
with its tea-cosy lid
and the porter
tugging his silent cargo.

No my friend
the hospital is not for me—
in my desktop world
Death is only a symbol
to be dealt with in words.

To Simon

I remember once
you were in the backyard
wearing my pyjamas—
for one bizarre moment
I thought you were me—
and it was I
standing in the darkness
coming out of the servant's room
hearing a noise
and walking to the window.
It was I
who looked in
at the white face—

"Is everything alright, Baas?"
"Yes," I said.
"Everything is alright now ..."

To Levi

When we saw the seagulls
I was secretly
sifting the year
through my fingers.

I played the white flutter
like a kite
letting it lift
and wheel
over the beach.

But the year
was heavy
in my hand.

I remembered
how my mother
draws me like a kite
tugging her cord
at my distance.

The seagulls rise
bursting into butterfly segments.

In the other dream
they are calling
my name.
The children are ready.
The cattle trucks open.
They are calling
my name.

I awake to find
I am standing on my name.
The words are set
in cement.
They are calling
my name
and I shout
I am ready!

Lifting like a kite
I float higher and higher,
railway tracks
like a ribbon
trailing
back to earth
to my name
cemented in another country ...

The seagulls rise
taking me with them.

Against the Time of Your Going

Like a squirrel
saving food for the winter
I am storing memories
against the time of your going.
I have taken your eyes
and your voice,
the way you use your hands
your heavy eyebrows
the way your eyebrows sing
their own kiddish ...
I will hang these memories
from a string
that in my winter
I will know its touch
against my chest.

To Bubbles

You place a labyrinth
between us.
To reach you
I must reach myself ...
Where to begin?
There is a river inside me.
A boat drifts.
On its deck
a boy holds a map.
A chart of rivers.
On one
a small boat is drawn.
A child
can just be seen
holding a page.

The pattern seems endless.
When a building dies
a shroud is erected
to hide the agony
of empty rooms
exposed to light.
What of my pain?
What can I raise
to hide this hollow
your eyes would open?
My love
you will have to accept me
as I am
concealed
and lost.
Your breast was asleep
in the core of my hand
in the calm of five fingers.
Like a flower
shielding the hidden womb
my palm cups its secret.

To Gillian (1)

I can hear her talking in her sleep,
calling out—
refusing the demands
made by her dream—

She cries softly

In the darkness
I can just make out
the profusion of auburn whirlpools
about her head.

She has found her thumb—
the dream accepts her again.

For Fran

who died at the age of 17

Isaac
bound on the altar
waiting for the miracle
that always comes ...
I place your trust
In a locket.
It hangs from my neck
like a stone.
For I am Abraham
bent by the weight
of your eyes.
Talk to me—
I want to forget
There are flowers
bursting from your pocket.

To Beatrice

This month
I wear my whiskers
with a pronounced droop.
Our summer birds
are leaving for Europe—
and Canada!
I am ringing a birdwatcher
who rings the birds—
They've had it all—more or less—
our beaches, our stumpy trees,
the politics, and a long hot summer.
And I
in my pasteurised chambers grow
my weeping willow moustache
aware that your winter-house
is changing
her dress for the occasion
and aware
that I can only hold
my end of the thread.
Careful not to pull—
or let go.

Lake Geneva

We meet in silence
like old lovers.
You are still as large
as my aloneness
and as cold.

Your boats still nudge
my darkest dream.

Beyond the mist
Evian lies asleep
and Arnold ...

I have only tears
for our meeting.

For Arnold

1.
At that moment
with Death knocking
I so wanted your Blessing.

And you offered it.

You looked at me
and for a long while
the whole world hung between us.
And I waited.

Oh God
could I only relive
that moment.
I sat
wanting your Blessing
but afraid
to acknowledge that Death
had opened the door.

Instead
I laughed away your fear
and I let the moment pass.
And Death sat by my side
on the bed ...

And now alas
the Blessing
is only mine to give—
"Thy sun shall never set
nor shall thy moon be withdrawn from thee."

2.
All night long you hover in my dreams
asking again for the words
I cannot bring myself to say.
Can I ever release you?
Your grave is now inside me
and I am with you alone
in the darkest cave I have ever known.

3.
Standing before the dark grey granite
reading for the thousandth time
the words—
as though it were something I had to do

to conjure you up—
I see you in shirt sleeves
leaning forward, heavy-chested—
your left hand taking the weight
on your left knee.
Always like this.
Pleased that I have come.
So much of you waiting
on the tip of my memory—
yet this is the image that always appears.
You in your shirt sleeves
tired at the end of a day.

It could be any one of a million moments—
you walking in the vineyards
hands high on your hips
frequently stopping to breathe,
and to listen to my endless talking—
or you walking on sand
the day blowing your hair wild
and your face red with sun—
and in one dark corner
of my memory
you when you died ...

When I come to visit you,
when I've read the ritual words
you come to me in your shirt sleeves
and you are always pleased to see me.

BOOK 2

Welcome to the Circus

(Justified Press, 1991)

For Jessica

Born on 14 December 1986

Welcome to the circus Jessie
You've missed nothing
arriving so late in the year.
All the acts reappear ...
Clowns
dressed like politicians
wag buffoon fingers
at the multi-coloured crowd.
You would be proud
and ashamed
of the toys and the games
men create
on the centre stage ...
in a high wire cage
blacks and whites
balance
and wait ...
In the darkness
only soldiers come and go.
Between
the sullen bear
and the lion show,
behind
the magicians
and the birds
that cannot fly,
God
is looking ...
Sweet innocent Jessica,
Welcome to the circus.

The Fish are Asleep

The fish are asleep.
Undressed,
they are stones
fragmenting
the green darkness.
The moon
sings them to sleep
in a shower
of silver shards.
My father floats
into my dream.
We are fish
in a glass bowl.
He drifts
stirring shadows
with empty hands.
I shout words
of love.
A kaleidoscope of silent bubbles ...
Your tongue
swims inside my mouth
like a small fish.
It plays hide-and-seek
with all my words.
I am lulled
into silence.

For Sheila (1)

I love you moon—
Moon-breast,
sleep-warm,
innocent in the dark palm-cradle.
Moon-thigh
silk-smooth
flowing
And always the secret
moon-forest.
Gently
I enter the calm circle
the blue-green fire,
the orange wheel
bursting
torn purple
round yellow
rising
in the endless night.

My Bicycle has a Basket

My bicycle has a basket
fixed to the handle-bars
for deliveries—
and for carrying little girls.
Don't be afraid—
I am cycling down
the main road
of your childhood.
Nothing has changed—
your doll's house whispers
while you sleep—
The bakery is breathing
the early morning bread—
even your father
large and as warm
as all your barefoot summers ...
You peep over the edge.
I know you are dreaming—
you are not aware
of the red dust
brown verandas,
the corrugated iron roofs—
There are only mountains
in your dreams—
and the wide river
you will cross as a woman.

Punch and Judy

He: My love
    Only your left
    hand
    in my right.
    A pact for the world.
    The shore contains
    the ocean.
    They move and grow
    together.

She: That hand
    shades my breast
    from pain.

He: I will love that
    breast
    with my mouth.
    An intimate pact—
    As clouds will nourish
    hills.

She: My heart
    wears that breast
    like a shield
    against pain.

He: I will hold
    that heart
    in my chest ...

She: And the pain
    my love—
    who will hold the
    pain?

The Windows of My Dreams

The windows of my dreams
are underlined
with snow.
Outside
the mountain-breasts
point their cold nipples
at a dark sky.
In one dream
mauve tears
weep into a lake ...

As a child
spinning off a sled
I rolled on an edge
of glass
staining the snow
with blood—
the pain froze
to my skin.

I would assemble my life
The wires, the poles,
the great, multi-coloured sail
ornate with words—
I would lift it all
without fear
and leap
into the yellow-smooth sky
of your paintings—
floating over breasts
and the dark forest
of your thighs.

The Flamingoes Pretend

The flamingoes pretend—
lounging on their flat rock
in their new pink shoes,
they know we are making love.
They fluff their dark velvet armpits
neatly into place—
poised on one leg
they pretend to be asleep.
I know they are listening
to our sighs—
They twist their sensual necks
deep into their tight white shirts
and smile ...

Walk Around Me

Walk around me
seven times
slowly
with great intent.
The first
and second
to give me time
to know
how beautiful you are.
The third
and fourth
for winding our Jerusalem
about my feet.
The fifth
and sixth
to bind our hearts.
The last path
brings you slowly
to my side.
Can you hear me?
I am whispering.
I love you.

So Early

So early
the birds whisper
in the sleeping trees—
so early, the mist
is still asleep
between the grey hills.
When you come
disguised as the sun—
you gently warm
the lids of my eyes
and my lips—
so early sun
so early loving—
my thighs are on fire.

My Gentle Love

My gentle love
I make you
a necklace of tears
Touching each centre
with sunlight—
a string of golden domes!
This is my anguish—
I bring you tears.
I pretend
they are poems ...

Lilith

Lilith, my dark wife
Cast your ancient spell—
You are the wild moon
in all my secret dreams.
You have stolen my child.
He is the candle flame.
He sleeps in the heart of flowers.
He lives and breathes
in your magic.

My Hunger

My hunger matches yours.
Count the rooms, and the windows—
Count the ceilings, and the beds—
Count the eyes,
and all the searching
all the voices, and the hands—
and count
the watching
and the waiting—
your ravenous tongue fits
my hungry mouth.

In Portofino

In Portofino
the boats are restless.
They nudge each other.
The houses sleep
in their antique masks.
They are old women
with painted faces
dreaming of love.
You appear in their dreams
you are a young girl
waiting for the mist
to lift
in Portofino bay.

Sheila in her Moon Phase

Not another moon.
Moonscape.
Moonrise.
Melancholic moon setting
in a flat sky.
A coy moon
snug between
the mountain's breasts.
A buoyant moon
floating
On an endless sea ...
If you have to paint—
paint me
making love to you.
Paint viridian whirlpools
of tongues and hands,

paint crimson,
paint madder—
paint the frenzy
of a cadmium sigh.
Paint us asleep—
like spoons—
The cerulean stillness
that always comes after—
But please
Sheila—
please—
not moons ...

Your Last Painting

Your last painting
is a portrait of me.
A Turneresque sky
burning to mist,
a burnished sea,
sweeping planes
of silence.
It's me in my sixtieth year ...
The conflict of passion
and stillness.
The struggle for grace.

The Passage of Birds

The birds lift and wheel
shaping the warm currents
that lift off the sea.
Remember
how we watched them
rise and gather
leaving the evening sky
and Israel
for their journey south.
Remember
holding hands
in Dizengoff Street
buying an ancient ring
to bind the days
and the nights
and the passage of birds
in a ring shape—
with no beginning
and without an end.

The Hills of Jerusalem

On certain nights
the hills of Jerusalem
stop singing.
The evening cups the ears
of all who sleep—
and God sits
on the hills
surrounded
by the whisper
of small wings.
On that night
the secret notes
in the Western Wall
turn to doves.
All the notes
except mine.
Instead of wishing
I wrote my fears ...

Shy Father

Shy father
I cannot be Isaac
knowing you are stretched
on the stone
at my side—
One of us
must hold the knife!

When I was a Kite

When I was a kite
lifting
above the red cloud
of my Mother's womb—
I knew the ache
the sweet longing
the cords tug in my stillness ...
I want to stand before you
naked.
I want to trace
again
that secret path—
this love that flows
from your breasts
to my lips—
from your sun
to that shade
where only my heart
casts a shadow.

Nothing Else to Do

There was nothing else to do
The dead were watching
We placed the flowers in position,
we whispered
and cried softly ...
The granite boats float in the rain
rocking the dead back to sleep.
There was nothing else to do.

Sheila Says

Sheila says
the dead return to us
as birds.
The dove that waits
at our window
is her father.
The nervous sparrows
are my parents.
They feed on their own
not letting me near.

Like Chinese Women

Like Chinese women
binding their daughters' feet,
my Mother bound our lives
with Sabbath candles
and braided bread.
Always
weaving the candle flame
through her hair
as she prayed,
and always
her eyes binding
our hearts
with ancient fear.

When Ancient Anatomists

When ancient anatomists
opened the heart
for the first time—
God was asleep
in the parachute cords
of the small valves.
A finding
of some moment
and much bewilderment—
not in a church
or a temple—
but here
between the soul's breath—
God lived in the ebb
and flow
of the blood's tide.

Like a Miner

Like a miner
and his canary
you carry a rose
into court
protection against lies
and the shabby truth.
Rivers run
and mountains tear apart
in silence ...
In the divorce court
marriages break
with the sound of a rose
closing.

Pharmacy

When I walk into your world
I still expect
the sweet brown smell of malt—
A splinter-edge of sulphur—
the ancient breath
of jars and paste
and coloured lotions.
You no longer cast
your waxy bullets
or grind the aromatic powders
and yet
an antique magic
lingers
on all the silent pots.

The Curtain Rises

The curtain rises.
On stage
the day begins.
The young girls
paint their faces.
The men gather
in the street,
Voices
and movement.
She is waiting in the wings.
A shadow
miming all the gestures.

For Levi

I will take my violin
to the highest point.
I will play
for all the empty windows,
the horizon of silent roofs,
for the cars
that speed under the bridge
unaware.
I will reconstruct the trees
and the water lilies
with my music.
I will pretend
I do not miss you.
I am only afraid of the wind
finding shreds of melody
on all the paths.

On Visiting Kaufering Outside Dachau

I walk in your forest.
The grey cement-bag
you wore
covers my body.
Behind me
an endless trail
of ashes
mark the path.
The forest denies everything.
Neither the flowers
nor the innocent grass
can cover
the cry
of ashes.

For Noelle

In my world
Sparrows nudge my daily bread.
In yours, seagulls
wheel and hawk for food.
The same wind sweeps
your ocean and my roof.
The same day hides
our separate dreams.
The same clouds weep
on both our lives.

I wear this pain
as a mark
on my forehead.

For Dan

The Philistine children cheer
as the child Goliath steps out
on the centre stage
in the school play.
He is heavy
in tin-foil armour.
Type-cast
for his booming voice.
He is about to shout
the five words
rehearsed for weeks.
Both the Philistines
and the Jews
are waiting.
A silence.
The children fidget.
Then a small voice
hesitant,
tearful,
a voice bathed
in sadness.
The death of his cat
swept away
the giant's roar—
and left the gentleness
of a grown man.

For Sheila (2)

Your breasts still cast
their gentle shadows
in my dreams.

Holding you while you sleep
I hear your heart beat
in the core of my chest.
The night sings to me.
The stars undress.
They sleep in the soft folds
of your thighs.

I am still in awe.

In this haphazard world
of desperate aloneness—
in the uncontrollable chaos
of living—
I found you.

On Seeing the Retrospective of Matthew Whippman

Shy man
your paintings rejoice!
I walk through your life
from dream to dream.
We are all
so serious.
You would have laughed ...
You taught me
the formula
for making grey.
Shades of grey
angled and spread.
One stroke—
a grey-white wall
burns.
A long sweep
spills
the morning mist
over grey-brown
green-grey earth.

In my heart's dark salon
I hang the grey silence
of your last painting.

For Tibor Lichtman

*(A survivor of Auschwitz, he had taken it upon
himself to visit Dachau daily, caring for the dead.)*

Tibor Lichtman
alone you whisper
the lullaby of Kaddish
in the silent camp.
Walking into Auschwitz
you remembered the story
of the boy
lost in the forest.
His tephillin* turned
into a bird
and he was saved.
Tibor Lichtman
secretly holding
the limp strands
of torn tephillin ...
Bind the darkness
through your fingers!
Wind the pain
and all the anguish
around your arm!
Let the sleepers
know
at last
a bird flies
out of your forehead!

** Strands of leather bound on the forehead, through the fingers
and around the forearm of the left hand during special prayers.*

For Lou

When the sea is dark
and brooding,
I think
of Gill and Tom
placing the ashes
and their tears
on the surface
of the water.
The incomprehensible
smallness
of all that remained—
and the endless ocean
of tears.

Song for Frank

"Avec le temps
Tout passe. Tout casse. Tout lasse."

All things fade
even in St James
in all that sun
and green—
green
like a moist birth
in every leaf—
you and I
were fading.

All things break.
A picture of you on a bridge
your beard breaking
an edge of sky—
your eyes splinter
the broken water.

Everything dies.

And we set you
down here
in our own hot earth.
In the early mists
wild birds will call—
in still summer nights
an African moon
will sing.

For Sheila (3)

The Crake Gallery Exhibition, Spring 1989

The Birth
    Heavy with oil
    feel
    how it kicks and struggles.
    Our entire life
    held in tiny canvas fingers ...
    And then the pain
    Pain fragmenting shafts
    of earth, and air, and water-sky
    melting green
    lightening blue
    the exquisite pain
    of sharp horizons.
    Behold
    the serene children
    smiling in their windows.
    They forget
    the agony
    of their birth.

First Child
    In the beginning
    there was dreamtime.
    Turtle-green currents
    hung in the cold air
    and God created silence.
    On the second day
    He created shadows.
    Aquamarine shadows
    of birds in flight.
    On another day
    wanting serenity

God painted the air gold
sheer as cobwebs.
When a man dies
his soul (which is woman),
white as an almond
floats forever
in a sea
of burnished mist.

Second Child
I am the silence
of a beach
remembered in dreams.
A red wind
shredding gold
on the shoulder
of a distant hill.

Chorus
We are reflections
of water.
The sea is painted on the sky,
mountains fold
in endless mist.

Third Child
Kaleidoscope of air.
Birds of Picasso
make love in flight.
Their feathers flash red
violent blue
orgasmic yellow.

Chorus
   We are reflections
   of light.
   The sky is painted on the sea.
   The waves steam
   teasing a warm silk
   in the purple air.

Fourth Child
   Brown days—
               and a sky
   stretching beyond God.
   The ocean
   like a warm hand
   smoothing a brown silence.
   My naked aloneness
   has vanished.
   I am the satin water
   caressing the soft-brown shore.

Fifth Child
   When the Oriole sang
   the morning was weightless
   a smudge of pink
   on water and sky
   a single liquid note
   rising
   in the dark mist.
   In another life
   in a dream half-forgot
   a forest awakes
   a shoreline draws silver
   from the greying edge of night
   and always

the golden Oriole
that one limpid call
falling
on soft shadows.

Sixth Child
Breathe in
shreds of gold.
Breathe out
the liquid shadows.
Listen
how the wind whispers
to the sleeping stones.
Mother of clouds,
chameleon of light.
Breathe in
the warmth
of hand and eye.
There is nothing else
Only love.

Chorus
We are reflections
Deep compounding reflections
of the soul.

BOOK 3

I See You

(Southern College Press, 2001)

I See You

"I see you," she said,
wiping apartheid from her eyes—
Standing tall
her small breasts reflecting
the gentle sweep
of her lower spine.
"I see you too," I say.
"I see you for the first time ..."
We reach out and touch
tentative, uncertain—
I am happy I can say
"Sikhona,
I am still here."

Homage to Women

1.
The dream begins.
In the darkest reach
of my sleeping soul
a curtain opens
and she is there
naked as water.
She is all breast
all mother
and with an ache I know
she is all woman.

2.
She unwound the snake
from her wrist.
He abandoned the memories
of Eden—
the fruits
and the flaming sword.
The soul
of the earth-mother
was there in her eyes.
They were unashamed
of her milk-white breasts—
the roundness
and the softness
of her hips.
She lifted herself
above his head
in balance.

3.

Her walk was languid—
heavy breasts and ample thighs—
voluptuous, naked—
smelling of earth and rain.
I drown
in the whirlpool
of shoulders and arms.

4.

She was dancing alone
Zaembekiko.
A dance for men—
for older men
who know the despair
of being men ...
The passion and the defeat.
She held her head high
like all Greek men—
She made no attempt
to hide her sex.
She thrust her breasts
proudly
filling the small room
with the smell of musk
and blood.
She sank to one knee
as men do—
She rose slowly
breathing darkness and sweat.
It was a dance for men—
the rhythm and the pain
was all woman.

5.
She thrust her tired breasts
as she walked—
her bottom
remembering an arrogance—
each step
lifting a roundness.
She is still afraid
of that dark orchid
flowering between her thighs.
Aphrodite forever ashamed
of the sensuous dream.

6.
Sensual
like a Georgia O'Keeffe flower
the red invites me.
I write poems
on your thighs
while you sleep.
Wild red poems
filled with turmoil
and love—
with dark clouds
twisting in a restless sky
with cloud-lakes pouring
steam and foam
and a Georgia O'Keeffe flower
singing.
I write poems
on your forehead
while you paint.

7.
The heavens undress.
The naked stars
whisper her name—
Goddess of night.
She alone can touch
the secret hurt
in the aching heart.
Weaving
her crown of shadows
she commands the soul,
the shrieking blood
the ancient crumbling bone.
At her command
the lemon moon turns the sea
into silver,
the trees and the sand
into stone.

8.
She stretches like a cat
Unwinding the tightness—
freeing the ebb and rush
of blood.
Her muscles breathe
the morning light.
When she stretches
she is the willow
arching in the gentle wind—
she is the ocean's slap and flood
when the tide wakes.
When she stretches
the shadows disappear.
The sun sings on her brown skin.

Objects in Space

Association of Art, Pretoria,
26 September 1988

1.
In the beginning
there was dreamtime.
Turtle-green currents
hung in the air—
and God created silence.
On the second day
He created shadows.
Aquamarine shadows
of birds in flight.
On another day,
wanting serenity,
God painted the air gold—
sheer as cobwebs.
When a man dies
his soul (which is woman)
white as an almond
gentle and round—
floats forever
in a sea
of burnished mist.

2.
I love you moon,
moon-breast,
sleep-warm,
innocent
in the dark palm-cradle
moon-thigh,
pale-smooth,
flowing

to the black
moon-forest.
Gently I enter
the calm circle,
the blue-green fire,
the orange wheel
bursting
torn-purple,
round-yellow
rising
in the endless night.

I Love You

I love you
while the moon drifts amongst
the sleeping stars
over Ixopo—
and I love you
when the distant hills
sketch their silhouette
on the morning sky.
I will sit on that ancient raft
in meditation—
I will fill the saffron sails
with my breathing.
The moon sits on my shoulder—
I am the horizon edge—
I am the dark trees—
Birds are dreaming in my hair—
floating in this silence
there is only love.

All Night

All night
the seagulls cried
outside my window.
The echo of your body—
the secret
imprints of your breasts—
Dreams—
Heavy with ocean and mist
the morning weeps.

My Love

My love
the waves have taken our footprints.
We are remembered.
The wind
etches our names
on small stones.
Asleep
your skin tastes
of the sea.
We have learnt to lock
our bodies.
The same ocean lifts and falls
in our dreams.

A Green Tide Breathing

A green tide breathing
Everything is naked.
The endless whisper
of a giant heart calling.
Your breasts invite me.
The nipples tease my lips—
The knotted gold
of my oldest dream
waits
in the shadows.

Have You Noticed

Have you noticed
how your toes
etch their image
in the soles
of your sandals?

I carry the imprints
of your fingers
on my chest.

Without You

Without you
a lonely alter-ego
asleep in the shadow
of my soul,
suddenly awakes.
In Montreal
a cold wind grabs
at my shirt—
I can smell the snow
of last year's winter
hanging
behind the low grey sky.
Dormer windows
brood
over quaint iron stairways
that spill
onto noisy streets ...
I am aware
of that me
reflected in all the windows—
the silent me
nudging an empty day.

Is it Your Breasts' Heat

Is it your breasts' heat
that draws my hand
in the cold bed?
Does it know
a nipple will wake
stretching itself—
trembling
into a wild
conflagration?
What secret mysteries
the fingers know ...

Sitting Before Me

Sitting before me
I watch her raise a bare arm
and touch her partner's back—
She was gentle—
her fingers lingered on his hidden spine—
At that moment
like a bird in flight
tugged by the earth's force—
I longed for home.

Karen McKerron Gallery, 1994

1.
In a brief splinter of space
I thought of bread—
The sweet heady scent of bread—
the smell of wheat
and earth
and a gentle breeze
running
like a golden tide
over angular fields
intersected again and again
by evening skies.
Closing my eyes
the Naples-yellow sings
of wheat
and wind
and wild dark currents.

2.
I can hear the giant stones waking—
lifting its mountain spine
through cloud-floods
breaking the ochre mist
brushing the light
in golden sweeps.

3.
I know that words can do this—
the right words
waking
the brooding fever
that it lifts and bursts
the even flow
of thought and dream.

This painting sets a stillness
inside me—
a deep brown silence
that always follows pain.

4.
Shadows
and a sweep of gold—
Strange how this roots me
binding my mind
and my soul.
I become the oil—
A mountain wakes—
a stone-edge lifts
in a draining mist
like sharp rock-spines
rising in an ochre flood.

Lament for Levi Shalit

1.
I am looking for you.
The moment
you walked away
you melted entirely
into shadow.
The moon could not find you.
All our stories—
those that were told
and those still to be told
hang in the darkness
between us.
I can hear the ocean.
It reflects my need—
even at night
the waves are searching,
sifting pebbles
and the fine sand.
I am looking for you.

2.
I will take my violin
to the highest point.
I will play
for all the empty windows,
the horizon of silent roofs,
for the cars
that speed under the bridge
unaware.
I will reconstruct the trees
and the water lilies
with my music.
I will pretend
I do not miss you.

I am only afraid
of the wind
finding shreds of melody
on all the paths.

3.
Who is this sleeping
safe in his Tallit? *
He carries the shadows of the camps
in his eyes
and in his hands.
His prayer-shawl
is a sail
drawing him silently
across the dark river.
He is an eagle
soaring in the clouds.
He is the singing of waves
on the sea that he loved.
Already he sleeps
like the ancient stones of Israel.

* *Jewish men are buried wrapped in their prayer shawls.*

For Clive

You belong to the men.
That ancient ritual
the blessing of men.
Strong arms will cradle
your wooden bed,
and always the voices
floating
above the stone forest
of this cemetery.
Blood-brother
you set fire to life
burning
the edges of will
and of love.
Then the astonishing silence.
The day crumbled
and turned to ash.
Now the blessings of men
sing you to sleep.

For Brett

I am mourning Brett
who came home
listening to the call of his heart.
The wind weeps
amongst the lonely trees—
the sun refuses to rise
on the dark horizon.
Brett is closing
the circle of his life.

For Hilda

Storm against the darkness!
Rage with every nerve
of your soul!
Hilda!
Resist the shadows' drag!
Deepening night
will drown
your laboured breath.
Hilda!
The cold wind
has found your heart!
Burst red!
Blood-red crying in the empty room!
Shriek red!

Then
the awful stillness ...

Gently Hilda,
Gently
let the silence
surround you.

For Jean

For a sculpting in her memory

Majestic and serene—
the wood floats on its ebony stand.
Now it is male
with echoes of power and musk
bursting on the gold skin-grain.
Now
it is woman—
a sweep of thigh
a proud arching of the neck.
There is always pain—
the shrinking of life and bone ...
Jean—
the wind sings!
The wild olive tree sings!
The twist and core of this wood-soul
sings!
You will be remembered!

Crake Gallery, November 1997

1.
You are a starling in flight.
A flash of red
a swoop of blue—
the sheer joy
of that blinding yellow—
a quickening wing
bursting
in a lilac sweep.
I watch you soar alone
unafraid.

2.
A celestial choir?
Angels and cherubs
playing their harps?
A spiritual harmony
heavenly blest?

Not a rolling of drums!
Not a crashing of cymbals
at the breath-holding crest!

I wonder about
the ancient enigma ...
What is the sound
of one hand
touching one breast?

3.
His fingers find her breast.
A soft curtain of moonlight
smoothes the weeping stars.

4.
Two smooth pebbles asleep
nodding in the shimmering stream.
Your breasts smile at me.

5.
Walk gently.
This is not canvas
or oil—
this is a journey
of the soul—
the hopes and the fears—
all the dreams of love—
a longing distilled
into silence.
Walk softly—
a butterfly is spreading
the paint
with its wings.

6.
Sheila opens the window
inviting the clouds
and the air
to breathe on her canvas.
She weaves the wind
into paint.
I stand in front of the picture.
The current flows
through my eyes
into my soul.

7.
Is this your hand or mine
squeezing my breast?
Is this love?

Will there be pain?
Is this your heart
or mine
calling?
I listen to the echo
of your touch—
I hold my breath
and wait ...

8.
I know Sheila's palette—
her canvases dream themselves
into paint.
She paints with light—
rays of green—
hot sweeps of magenta
and gold.
Sheila paints with air.
A bird could fly
between the streams of colour
and not touch
or disturb
the paint's breath.
She paints with pain—
I've seen her weep a darkness
on the cold canvas face—
a shriek of anger
sparking a burning white—
Sheila paints with silence.
Her paintings meditate
in an endless sea of calm.
I know her palette.
I know how her soul
paints itself
again and again.

Pictures at an Exhibition

Moussorgsky

I would use a cello
and a guitar—
nostalgic, limpid and dark
the cello would explore a single note.
The guitar
an urgent undercurrent
would let the cello
float alone.
I would create
a haunting feast of sound—
instead—
I bring you poems ...

For Clem and Clive

Under milkwood
the bride
in her veil of cloud
watched
her shy lover
balance the moon
in his eye—
under milkwood
the candles sang
to soft guitars
only love
only dreams
under milkwood—
under heavy scented milkwood
under the dark and sleeping milkwood.

For Benjamin

Benjamin
our own small Buddha—
we bring you gifts
to mark your birth
and the giving of your name—
lilac cluster grapes
of wild wisteria—
and the secret heady breath
of jasmine.
Benjamin
son of my right arm—
each year we will know you
with symbols of innocent joy.

For Talia

Born 2 February 1995

After the storm—
after the long night waiting—
The dew sparkles
splinters of sun
on leaf and grass.
Talia
Out of the shadows—
out of our deepest dream—
cradled in pain and joy—
a burst of light
of gold
of innocent love.
Talia.
You hold our hearts
in your tiny hands.

For Max

Max Erwin—
the names echo
the lives of men
who loved
and were loved
much as we now
love you.
You carry their memories
and their souls
in your amazing eyes.

On Meeting a Matthew Whippman

Taffy!
At an exhibition of flowers
your painting smiled at me.
I recognise your palette.
A smidge of white
the essence of roses—
a green-grey sweep
for air and space—
the suggestion of a vase
and for the base
the merest dream of blue.
I am again
in the hot sun of your life
laughing as we did
while music filled your canvas.
Then I remembered
you are no longer here ...

For Margy and Richard

The noon-day gun
thumped its minute cloud
at the peak of Signal Hill
marking again
the confluence of space
and time
that binds our lives.
No matter how you shaped
your life in Boston—
on the other side of the world—
we were waiting for you
on Table Mountain
where the noon-day
cannon
calls the time.

For Rachel

Rachel lives in a cocoon.
She is obsessed
with the endless tangle
of silken threads.
When will
she discover
she is a butterfly?

Behold the Irises

Behold the irises
as you enter Ixopo.
They bind their petals
in the candle posture
and meditate.
Sedate miniature Buddhas
solemn and silent.

In the lonely hours
when the dark mist
winds her fingers
through the sleeping trees
the irises wake—
unfolded
they are snowflake butterflies
dancing—
the moths
dreaming of love
leap and wheel
tossing
the night's pollen
in the soft sweet air.

Behold the irises—
they are living
double lives.

For Gillian (2)

The morning enters my dream—
Seagulls and the ocean breathing
beneath my window—
I wake thinking of Gillian—
how surprised she was
that I knew the name of a flower ...
an unbelievable, inconsequential moment
in her entire childhood
and our life—
What games are played
in the synaptic forest
of our brains!
The sadness—
the overwhelming nostalgia—
a tidal backwash of memory.
Weeping
I enter the morning—
Waves breathing under my window
and the seagulls' crying.

My Barber

My barber talks to me ...
He is an abused man
living with his fear.
My energy
And my strength
leave me
with each snap of his shears ...
I know
Psychiatrists lie on each other's couches
crying.
But who cuts the barber's hair?
Who listens?

On Hearing Arab Music

A night without stars.
Spirits rise out of the sleeping Nile—
the rhythm calls them.
In my deepest core
there is an echo—
the earliest sound—
an ancient cry.
It is my soul
singing.

Figures in Sand

Figures sculpted in sand.
A woman and a man.
The wind blurs the edges
leaching the granules.
He is the tide
devouring the mysterious shore.
She is the earth
melting.

Feathers

There are feathers
on the tips of my fingers—
I am the white crane
spreading its wings.
The clay struggles.
It refuses to become
a bird ...

For Masha

Again—
a bowl of stricken roses
bleeding
on a small table ...
trying to say goodbye ...
taking your hand ...
and again
reliving that moment
hoping
for a different end ...
When I arrived
the gardener
was pruning roses.
When I left
the roses
were gone ...

Yom Ha'Zikaron*

I am crying in the market.
The birds are silent.
The wind holds its breath.
Even the ocean has stilled
the restless thrust
of her waves.
Over everything
a siren is weeping.
The white lamb that waits
under the cradle
is weeping.
Israel is mourning her dead.

* *Israeli day of Remembrance for the Holocaust*

Like a Stone

Like a stone suspended in space
Jerusalem floats in my soul.
This is the secret dream we share—
an ancient lullaby—
a memory in blood—
golden stones
that weight us to this earth
generation after generation.

Poems for Table Mountain

Exhibition at the Crake Gallery,
March 2000

1.
The first ship was a ghost
appearing out of cloud
and empty sea—
Then they came
nuzzling their wooden noses
in the leeward thigh
of the mountain's lap—
bringing their dreams
and the pain
of an old world.
The flat top beacon
became a window
into the dark soul of Africa.

2.
The wind dropped,
the towering waves
faltered
and were still—
our small wooden world
floated
between the wind's breath
and the uncertain ocean—
And it was there
rising out of the sea!
Africa is anchored
at its tip by a peg
beaten flat—
it stops the continent
drifting ...

What I saw
was God's anvil—
massive clouds
thundering
on the sharp edge.

We drifted closer
the solid silence
of its immense sides
rising—
no longer a silhouette
on the edge of the world—
but a brooding
giant—
the next moment a mystical
cloud-swept dream
gathering shadows
into its core.
I am
this tiny wooden boat
afloat
on an endless sea.
My compass-heart
is locked
on Table Mountain.

3.
Behold the mountain
it is the mirror of your soul.
The stones brood—
dark shadows drain
the rock's face.
The mists weep—
the wind shrieks its pain
in the deepest cleft.
The trees hum

lifting a green stillness
on the calm granite wall.
The mountain laughs
dancing birds call
in the sparkling sun.
Table Mountain
it is the mirror of your heart.

4.
We have climbed this mountain
You and I
bending
to the twist and stretch
of the path and gravel edge—
Clouds dance at our feet.
The vast ocean
hangs from the horizon
a shimmering curtain
of light
and deep ultramarine.

5.
Table Mountain at night
the massive stones are asleep.
They are dreaming
of purple
and deep umber.
The seagulls
tired of pacing the restless ocean
nestle in the dark crimson folds
of the mountain's dream.
The bay is silent.
A cloud bank waits in the shadows—
it is afraid to breathe.
Table Mountain is asleep.

6.
There are days when Table Mountain
is a cardboard prop
held in place by a cable.
A flat backdrop
to a busy week.
On other days it is there
in my soul—
the eternal icon—
my towering Buddha
marking my heart's stillness.

7.
In the cleft of the mountain's thighs
deep in her secret forest
we clambered—
the dark ferns—
the heavy wet sweetness
of green ...
the half-leaf begonia
blushed in the shadows.
Slowly,
step by step,
we walked the year's trail
to its end.

8.
The air is heavy with rain.
Table Mountain floats.
One moment it is there
a silver spirit hiding in the mist.
Drenched and drained
of all colour
it blurs into sky,
into cloud,
into water.

9.

Driving down from Franschhoek
we watched the sun run havoc
between the fleeing clouds
setting fire
to the fleece and lining
until the entire sky
burnt scarlet
burnt gold.
In all this
Table Mountain remained
serene and cold
sharp-edged in the dying light.

10.

In the entire mystic woof
and warp
of this hot tapestry—
this Africa
with its brilliant light
and terrible darkness—
with all the ancestral mists
and common mysteries—
there is one icon
a flat-topped table-top mountain
nature's giant hand
holding up the sky.

BOOK 4

I Dreamt I was Flying
(Nimrod Publishers, 2007)

I Dreamt I was Flying

I dreamt I was flying.
A silent wind
raking my hair
as I
swoop
into my childhood ...
my father
is smoking a cigar—
the scent of rum
and maple
fill the dream—
my mother
is baking bread—
I float
in the sweet cinnamon warmth.
I dreamt I was crying—
Tears
billowing
around me.

My Entire Life

I have written my entire life
on the inner surface
of your thighs.
There are poems
on the palms of each hand—
On the soles
of your feet
all my secret dreams.
My joy of waking
at your side
is etched
on your forehead.

My Father Hides

My father hides
in my mirror.
"Why are you here?"
I whisper.
"You should be asleep
in that other world."
He looks at me
with tired eyes.
He never speaks.
I recognise the silence.

Sandpipers

The gentle yin
seeps its frothy edge
into the sand
and wells back
into the immense
core of the sea.
The angry yang
slaps the beach
and races
to the furthest rim.
Sandpipers know
the unstoppable rhythm.
With a blurring of frenetic
matchstick legs
they chase the melting yin
and desperately flee
the surging yang.

We are
all
sandpipers
in this ebb and flow
of living ...

Poems for an Exhibition of Sheila's Paintings

1.
Bungee jump with me.
Poised on the lip
of the gossamer edge—
Hold your breath
and leap
eyes and heart
stretched wide
and open—
Leap
through the timeless
flat-blue, cotton-blue,
shredding-blue
funnel of light.

2.
Ankles jerk
as you yo-yo
down the dazzling white
falling and rising
the transparent green
and the plaintive green
lift and fall.

3.
Pierneef could touch
such a sky—
Whispers of mauve,
shafts of lilac-green—
on a splinter of air.
The gauzy purple thins.
After the first crash
of Genesis—
This is the way the world begins.

4.
I watch you asleep.
The beds of your nails
are blue.
Yesterday,
they were green.
You are a kaleidoscope
of life
with your hands plunged
in the pulse
and the colour
of living.

5.
Hanging upside-round
in the dip and sway
of the bungee cord
I feel the secret drag
of a recent loss.
Wrapped in her shadow
a dead mother watches.
In the grey silence
I can hear her voice.
On the second turn
of bungee space
I am once again
in the warm flow
of fragmenting light.

6.
I float in a green nimbus
of multi-coloured air.
The sepia mountains melt—
Time clamps
pain and love
in tight black sheets
of memory.

The cord twists.
Scaffolds of colour
criss-cross the rising mist.
Joy and sadness.
Rivers etched in fire—
Mountains weep
and meld
into yellow-brown streams.

7.
Once in meditation
I bungee jumped
into the mystic art
of Sheila's dream.
The serene sweep of valleys
filled my soul.
For a stillness in time
I was the cloud
Suspended
in a bouquet of light—
I was the silence
flowing
from canvas to canvas.
Come—
jump with me!

Dialogue with Sheila's Painting

"Is it silent?"
        "It is always silent
        in the beginning."
"Will there be mist?"
        "The earth is cradled
        in mist at the moment of birth.
        The sun comes later,
        discovering its heat
        as it lifts."
"Are there people?"
        "This is the silence
        before there are eyes ...
        This is the way
        the earth begins."

A Poem About Fire

"Write a poem about fire," she said
An African fire—
darkness and sea."
I stand before
this small canvas—
the oils crackle
and burn—
the heat
scorches my face.
A rage
pent-up smouldering
erupts!
The flames curl
searing my brain
and all of my life ...

The Mist

The mist came slowly
using the night—
an ocean of mist
filling the valley
drenching the mountain's edge
in cloud.
I remember the whiteness
and the silence—
The night's stillness
woven in mist.

Sheila's Painting of the Drakensberg at Sunrise

Standing
in this canvas,
I can hear the mist—
the cold air rising.
I tighten the laces of my boots—
I am ready.

I talk to the stones—
on the narrow paths
that stitch
the grass to the mountain's chest.

I wait for your mountain
to wake.

Climbing the Drakensberg

Celebrating the miracle
of shadows—
the ever-changing web
etched
on the white rock face.
Waking with the sun.
Tent-pegged on a shelf—
a busy rumbling stream—
and the Drakensberg
breathing ...
Celebrating the horizon shift.
Not the sea—
Not the healing bush—
Not forests
heavy with scented bark—
But here
on the world's roof
hearing the silence
of the soul.

We came to a cleft of rock.
God's window
in a mountain cathedral.
I heard the sun
bursting fire
in an African sky—
The roar of light
on the horizon edge—
The burning valley
shouting a dark green
in a shimmer of heat.
The sounds filled my eyes.
You heard it in your soul.

Spionkop

This morning I climb Spionkop
with the British.
It is the 24th of January
in the year 1900.
We are floundering in mist ...
In desperation
we dig trenches—
Later, at leisure,
we dig graves ...
I am also with the Boers
hiding on the far lip
of the hill
waiting for the sun to rise ...
On this acre of hallowed ground
the names of all the Boers
and the Brits ...
The wind stirs
the wild African grass.

(Drakensberg. 1 January 2002)

Yiddish Lullaby

I am searching
for my mother's voice.
Behind
the angry tears
I hear her singing.
She is singing.
Rozhinkes mit mandlen.
My name
is woven
into the song.
Rozhinkes mit mandlen.
A white goat
is asleep
under my cradle.
Rozhinkes mit mandlen.

A Single Rose

A single rose sits on my desk
listening.
She's clearly embarrassed.
Talking about love
makes her blush.
A deep arterial glow—
spreading dark magenta
at her core.
Secretly, I'm envious.
I can't remember
such innocence,
and it's far too late to pretend.

Dark Gondolas

Dark gondolas
lashed to slender poles
looking solemn
in their blue winter hoods.
The backwash
of passing boats
leaves them
dancing
in the grey-green mist.
Remembering
You and I
in Venice,
my gondola heart
dances
in the backwash
of memory.

On the Naming of Paintings

For Sidney

We walked into their flow
and their
rhythm.
We touched
the blue-green air—
caressed
the gentle
sweep of light.
The forms without shadows
and the towering skies.
One by one
softly
the paintings whispered
their names.

For Sidney and Monty

On the opening of their exhibition

Walk softly.
The paintings
are deep in meditation.
Even the air is still.
A dialogue
of coloured mist.
I tiptoe
into the museum
of the soul.

Walk slowly.
A kaleidoscope
of singing light—
Transparent glass
transposed on green
on blue
on air—
a spiral of song
reflecting life.

For Sheila (4)

Even now
I am at your side
discovering the forms
and functions
of Chicago's high-rise world.
We breathe in harmony
when Ben says
"Don't leave me."
I have the same pain
at the same moment
in the same
secret
heart space.

For Ferruh Simsek

My friend
you will have to learn
the ancient trick
of distant loving ...
Secretly stretching
your heart's shadow ...
This is not for the young.
The ability
comes with age ...
You will work—
You will talk to friends—
You will eat—
And you will sleep—
You will never stop feeling
that your soul
is on the tip
of your nose ...

For Gillian (3)

I think of Montreal
a sudden Arctic wind—
and the day falling
into darkness—
heavy clouds
and the cold sharp scent
of rain—
then you left ...

For Marc

Born 22 September 2001.
Underwater birth.

1.
Hello!
Can you hear me?
This is your grandfather
speaking.
I want to tell you
I love you.
It's time for you
to come out ...
By the way—
I hope you can swim ...

2.
All my life I have waited
secretly dreaming
of electric trains
extravagant kites
plastic guns
and trim lead soldiers ...
I have grown weary
of Barbie dolls
and sewing sets ...
I am waiting for a small boy
with his cricket bat
or a magic pirate sword ...
Now you have arrived
I can only cry ...

For Sheila (5)

On the birth of her first grandchild

The autumn sun
danced in your eyes
while you listened
to Benjamin
on the other side of the world.
Benjamin saying
with his first cry—
"I am here!"

For Benjamin

Born May 2001

Benjamin asleep on his father's chest—
a fragile transition—
bathed in the sounds of his mother's breast—
he listens at last
to the rhythm of men ...
Benjamin
in all your dreams
your soul will return
again and again
to the comfort
of a woman's heart.

For Morrie

On walking in downtown Chicago

Halstead Street,
Wabash Avenue.
Each day a memory is caught
on the hook of a dark
subterranean cord,
a fragment—
a nostalgic tug.
I am trawling my past.

For Sarah

Your chestnut hair
is a miniature waterfall—
a million whirlpools
and eddies—
golden shadows dance
in the twist and leap
of brown currents.
A wild cascade
of magic curls!

Paris

1.

Innocent Buddha
serene and alone.
Time has stripped
the Burmese teak
to its grain—
its image blurred
by centuries
of rain.
Walking the narrow streets
of Paris
I heard this Buddha
whisper my name ...
An ancient Buddha
torn from his forest.
Later
listening to Vivaldi
in a darkened church
I could still hear
the Buddha's voice.
I'm not sure
if it's my voice
or a lonely Buddha
calling ...

2.

Maillol's model
Dina Vierny
cast in bronze.
Petulant lips
like Cupid's bow
uncertain, hesitant,
inviting.

We stare
into each other's eyes—
your entire being
comes alive.
It is I
who turn to stone ...

3.
A jigsaw puzzle of roofs—
the angled
sharp-edged chimney stubs
thrusting
a kaleidoscope
of muted reds and raw sienna.
Listen.
The roofs are singing—
a rhythm of ochre
and shimmering slate.
This is the Paris
that comes to me
in my dreams.

Eclipse

The moon bleeds.
Smoky magenta,
and blood.
The weight of the earth's shadow.
This heavy earth—
This tear-drenched
heavy earth.

Portofino 2005

Nothing has changed.
Not the houses—
not the boats
dancing in the bay—
Under an awning
a poet still sits
writing
about love and dreams ...
Time is asleep
in Portofino.

Victoria Falls

The river hears
the ocean's call—
the relentless
tidal pull—
In the surge
the reflection
of trees disappears—
Even the sky
melts—
The elaborate mist
laced
in a rainbow
refuses to leave.

Numbers

I am burdened
by numbers—
cell numbers
phone numbers
dates of birth
and ID numbers.
My military name—
my bank
and all those secret numbers ...
passwords
zip codes
and personal PIN numbers ...
I am regimented
and catalogued—
the history of my life
my tax returns—
where I go
and how I travel
filed away in endless numbers ...

Sydney

Everything is diminished
by the deep lonely cry
of the didgeridoo.
The Opera House,
its white circular sails,
the elegant bridge
criss-crossing light and space ...
the boats, the buildings
and all the people.
This prehistoric call
shrinks the entire world.

Haikus for Tai Chi

At 7am the Tai Chi class meets. Week after week. Month after month. Through all the moods and changes of the season. The Dojo has a wall almost entirely of glass. We can see green fields and trees. They are part of the Dojo. They enter the Tai Chi form.

These Haiku poems grew out of the energy and spirit of each morning.

Haiku for January
Birth of a new year.
We float in the Chi-drenched hall.
Cut grass. Scent of summer.

Haiku for February
The same class. Sinking
Chi into the tantien.
Sun rising in flames.

Haiku for March
The sun soaked in rain
refuses to rise. Chen swords
support the dark sky.

Haiku for April
The ten thousand things
begin by gathering Chi
from the silent trees.

Haiku for May
With the dignity
of an ancient Samurai—
The wood Tai Chi sword ...

Haiku for June

The class is silent.
Sifu demonstrates the form.
The trees stop breathing.

Haiku for July

The frozen sun hides
behind the lattice of naked trees.
The Tai Chi dream begins.

Haiku for August

Embrace the tiger.
Raucous hadeda spike the
early morning bugs.

Haiku for September

Balanced and silent—
Reeling silk from a cocoon.
The sun warms my face.

Haiku for October

A shaft of warm sun.
The breath of spring on my face.
Grasp the sparrow's tail ...

Haiku for November

Tai Chi. The hot sun
sweeps the night's rain. Silent dance
in a burning mist.

Haiku for December

There is no end. There
is no beginning. The truth
is in the silence.

Riga

Biekernieku Forest
(Site of the murder of 200 000 Jews)

1.
Only the sound
of rain
on the leaves.
The trees
are silent.
The jagged stones
are silent—
Listen—
Below the surface
The entire forest
weeps.

2.
Surreal forest.
The sun smiling.
A breath of light
caressing
autumn leaves—
But there are no birds ...
The dead curl
in the twisting roots—
The dead whisper.
They are everywhere.
And
there
are
no
birds ...

3.
A million fingers
pointing
at a blood-red sky ...
In my dreams
the earth is alive
with voices.
Women's voices.
Children crying.
Riga
your forests
tear at my soul ...

A poem for Quinne

On reading her poems

I want to stomp dance
around a fire—
The moon
Braving the ravenous clouds—
brushing aside
the glances of all the stars—
I will stomp myself into silence—
Into a sense of oneness
even with the moon—
And you will appear
heavy with smoke and sand-dust.
I will recognise you
by your heart-wrenching
sensitivity—
We will stomp around this fire
reciting poems
and crying.

For Dan (1960–2005)

1.
Curled
like two spoons
sleeping—
a dark butterfly wakes.
It flutters
in the warm clasp
of hand and breast.
The divine unconscious soul—
this secret Mother—
this other self

that cannot rest ...
On the other side of the world
Dan is waking.
Gently,
softly,
a butterfly hovers
above his head.

2.
Already
your proud head
is carved
in dark marble—
the silence
and the loneliness
of marble.
The storm is over.
The suffering
and the secret pain ...

3.
Holding her shattered heart
in her fingers—
she tore
his old T-shirt
into memories—
each fragment
drenched in his life.
I offered my token
to the lake—
the gentle waves
lapping at our feet ...
Dan is swimming.
He is asleep
in the soothing rhythm—

The water he loves
envelops him
washing away
the pain
and the darkness ...

4.
With one sweep
the entire sky
the desert
and the stillness
around us—
you offer Dan
to the Negev,
to a distant grove
of trees asleep
in the heat,
to the grey scrub
and lonely acacia.
The desert wind
will know him
Forever.

5.
Sheila wrestles with the Angel.
I hear them struggling.
They cry with rage—
Even the darkness weeps.
The inevitable memories
and the terrifying anger.

Sheila's Tree

For that mystic place
where Sheila and her counsellor
meet
each week.
I imagine Sheila saying:
I have often had a relationship
with trees.
This tree is different.
It sees through me.
Through all my pretences—
My attempts to feel normal ...
We met
when I was in the depths
of my loss.
It was bare.
More than bare.
It was stricken.
There was a terrible silence.
Birds avoided the tree.
Even the wind—the all-loving wind—
held her breath ...
The tree—and at that moment
I believed
only the tree
understood my loss ...
The tree was there
in my core,
and I was reflected
in every shattered branch.
I didn't think either of us
would make it.
Slowly.
Painfully slowly.
The way grief-time stops ...

I watched a whisper of green
appear.
I was jealous
and angry
that my tree had found
its own life-force—
I could hear the green.
The air holding my tree
turned green.
An innocence.
An uncomplicated simplicity.
A sudden abundance.

Now there are moments—
soft secret moments—
I feel
a faint blush of green
growing
inside me ...

For Sheila's Painting

In Memory of Dan, 2005

I refuse to believe
the burning of sky and cloud—
I refuse to believe the pain—
the fever of a day's heat
bleeding crimson—
I refuse to believe
the weeping sweeps of shadow
and the terrifying silence.
On another horizon
the dawn is breaking ...

BOOK 5

Late Harvest

When I see your face

When I see your face—
even now
in the late harvest
of this mysterious life,
my heart remembers
the hop
skip
and jump
of all our meetings ...
When you take off
your clothes
to lie at my side,
every cell and fibre
of my being
still
holds its breath.

Poetry Festival in McGregor

Wayward
South-Easter
be gentle.
Birds
are making
their nests
with words.
The trees
in McGregor
are heavy
with fruit.

Saturday, 25 April 2020

We are making love.
We are laughing.
We burst into each day
with joy
and a magical intensity.
Lying in bed,
I suddenly discover
I can
Feel the lower edge of my liver
in my abdomen.
I can feel a hard mass.
I am suddenly reminded—
Hey you're supposed to be dying ...
The room gets darker and colder ...

Goddess of Night

The heavens undress.
The naked stars
whisper her name—
Goddess of night.
She alone can touch
the secret hurt
in the aching heart.
Weaving
her crown of shadows
she commands the soul,
the shrieking blood
the ancient crumbling bone.
At her command
the lemon moon turns the sea
into silver,
the trees and the sand
into stone.

Listen

Listen
to the heartbeat
of the drum—
The great Nguni cattle
are whispering.
We have stretched
their souls
over the face
of the moon.
The moon
is singing.
Songs of darkness—
Ancient rhythms—
Stories
from the beginning of time.

Obituary

I keep looking
for my obituary
in the *Wits Review.*
Curious.
A paragraph?
An entire page?
Will anyone smile
at my age?
This for sure
when life demands
so be it—
I'm not dying to see it ...

My Mother's Voice

After all this time—
the resentments and the anger—
the coming to terms—
the acceptance of loss—
I am suddenly assailed
by my mother's voice
singing a lullaby.
There is a tenderness
and a caring
that I had forgotten ...

Such a Question ...

And God said
"Adam *knew* Eve."
One cryptic
apocalyptic word.
A sanction for loving?
To lose oneself
in a glorious moment
of ecstasy.
Would the world
have changed
if God had said:
"Now Adam
understands
Eve ...?"

Boggomsbaai Wedding

Only love
can shelter us
from life—
Ten thousand angels
will be there.
They never miss
a fairy-tale wedding.
They will be everywhere.
In Lize's eyes,
in the tips of Henk's fingers.
They bring
the blessings
of love.
Only
love
can shelter us
from life.

First Night in Intensive Care Unit, July 2017

At night
the high-care machines
talk to each other—
Lonely birds—
Pigeons
hiding their fears
in endless chatter—
While I
curled in my secret nest
listen
to the darkness
and wonder ...

Velvet Words

Velvet words
describe
the magic journey
my fingers take
discovering
your breasts.
The nipples wake
to butterfly touch.
The silk flow of your back
to that dark cleft—
the feather forest ...
Asleep at my side
I melt into
your dreams.

Lemon Tree

A lonely lemon tree
honours our Dan.
I can hear it
singing
in the darkness.
The flowers are asleep.
The pebbles surrounding
the plants
are asleep.
In the stillness
only the night breathing
and the plaintive voice
of a lonely lemon tree
singing.

Waiting

Brown days
and a sky stretching
beyond God.
The ocean
like a warm hand
smoothing a brown silence.
I am the satin water
caressing
the soft brown shore.
I am the sky
waiting
in silence.

Lightness

Children understand
Tai Chi.
The capacity to float
is built in.
They have butterflies
in their fingertips.
We have to reclaim
a lightness—
Seek out the tired
butterflies
hidden in our souls.

At the Entrance of the Tai Chi Dojo

It is there waiting.
A red bishop bird
quivering
on the fragile tip
of the tall grass.
A flash of blood
on the mat-green world.
Tai Chi
and the promise
of a new day.

Waking with the Sun

Waking with the sun.
Tent-pegged on a shelf—
a busy rumbling stream—
and the Drakensberg
breathing ...
Celebrating the horizon shift.
Not the sea—
Not the healing bush—
Not forests
heavy with scented bark—
But here
on the world's roof
hearing the silence
of the soul.

Saying Goodbye

I had words
with the tree.
The South African protea
we planted in Be'er Sheva
where the desert
still hugs the streets
and breathes
on all the windows.
We had words—
I know the sadness
of growing
in a strange soil—
the loneliness—
the sense of alienation.
So we had a few words
before we left ...

Yom Kippur

There is a massive silence.
The clocks stop.
No-one breathes.
He beats his chest
with his right hand.
He is crying.
His tears
float at his feet.
He is asking
forgiveness
for the sins
of commission.
For all the sins
of omission.
He opens that sacred book
where all the names
are carefully inscribed.
The dream ends.
I never get
to see God's face.

On Making a Ceramic Bowl

I hold the scent
of fruit
on the tips of my fingers ...
the heady musk
of swollen figs,
the sweet green touch
of lemon ...
My whole being
has to resonate
with the shape
the clay has to know
in its essence ...
I whisper
"fruit"
to the hollowing shape ...

Listen

Listen—
A purple Buddha
is laughing.
When the fairy-tale mist
clouds your vision—
when sharp-edged rain
drenches your very soul—
when even the moon
withdraws her light
and the painful night
seems to go on
forever—
a serene
implacable
eternally joyful
purple Buddha
is laughing.

Requiem

At the sea's edge—
where he ran ...
Where we
scattered
His ashes ...
Today
the sun is reluctant
to disturb
our solemn silence.
His daughter
with the magic wisdom
of childhood
touched him ...
A single lonely balloon
rising
in the grey light ...
Carrying the message
"Daddy
I love you."

The Hindu Wedding Dance

The sari absorbs the subdued lighting—
radiates a golden aura.
They all veil their faces,
seducing us
with hips and arms.
They sculpt the air
with fingers and hands,
tantalisingly move away
swaying
dipping and rising—
a magical intimacy.
They are weaving a spell.
They are dancing for the bride.

Candle

The comfort
of a candle flame.
Beyond the rituals,
beyond the many
festivals of light—
there is always
a single candle
burning
in the darkness
of our souls.

Saturday Night Fever

"At my table I declare
one famous sculptor."
"Ha!" you said.
"I have one poet."
"Not enough," I said.
"I have two Queen artists
exhibiting at this moment."
"Ha!" you said,
"I have a saxophone-player."
Drawing trumps
just like that.

And we played out
the evening while the lights lasted.
And cool jazz
filled our plates.

Wedding

It was love that
enticed
the moon
to our table.
There was love
in the speeches.
It was there
in everyone's eyes.
The moon walked
over the sleeping
ocean.
She sat at our sides.
She caressed the food
and our faces.
I am blessed.
An old man
weeping
in a flood of love.

The Play of Water

The play of water—
water
on stones—
water dancing
on water—
water completing
the balance
of space and light.
How these dreams
magically weave
the intimate fabric
of our lives ...!

The Moon and the Ocean

The moon and the ocean
are in love.
Night after night
the ocean sings
to the moon.
A song of wind
waves
and dark shifting shadows.
The naked moon
silent and serene
smiles.

The Sleeping Mountains

The sleeping mountains
are the first
to greet the rising sun—
The shadows
tiptoe away.
Even
the reluctant dark
in the mountain's lap
floods with light.
This is the story
of life.
Suddenly
the sun is everywhere ...

For Joe

Today
I will walk in your shoes.
I will know
the weight you carry
in your darkness.
The way it tugs
forever
at your soul ...

But the amazing warmth!
The lifting joy
of a new life!
Every step
is filled with wonder!

For Pauline

I need to share
a secret—
You know
that Sheila
loves you—
What you don't know
is that I live
in her skin.
When she breathes out
I breathe in.
We are one smile
and shed the same tears—
We are one body
with two names.
So you must know
when the sun rises
and the moon goes to sleep
I also
love you.

For Marinette

This is Marinette's necklace—
In her last breath
she knew
how
to untie the knot
in her mind's shadow—
the sudden stillness
the heart's peace.
The silver remembers.

For Marcelle

I am thinking of the marks
we made
on the wooden doorways
of your childhood years.
Always
standing straight
and always
so serious—
A secret stairway
for angels' feet ...

For Monty Sack

Gather cloud
and the air between.
The essence of trees,
the autumnal pain,
and the dark curling
green
at the earth's core.
Add a whisper
of man.
The volume
and silence of stones—
Let the giclée seep
its magic
distillation.
The white
universe
comes to life
and sings!

For Sheila (6)

We are Siamesed
by the heart's hip
and the soul's thigh.
Impossible to know
where your body begins,
or my arms end—
finding that other self.

For Sheila (7)

You are the moss covered
earth—
the bird song
and morning mist
of a river bank.
At night
naked as a fish
the water kisses
your shadow eyes
and I sleep
curled
in the gentle flow.

For Mary

In outer space
our cries continue
their journey
between the stars.
our tears spill
into vast oceans.
The universe cradles
our grief.
Like an ancient mythological
Priest
I stand
on the cliff's edge
holding the space
between pain and darkness
in my hands.
I would bless
your home
with love.

For Graham

1.
Listen—
The unmistakable
dance
of ice cubes—
Night has curled
her fingers
around
your heavy armchair—
The restless ocean breathing—
And always
the gentle rataplan
of ice cubes
on a glass wall.

2.
You have finally come home.
We have set you
asleep
in the haunting scent
of ancient earth.

Sipping wine—
While you watch
an Israeli moon
lift herself
into a kibbutz sky ...

Like a cupped hand
protecting a candle flame
we will hold you
forever
in our hearts' core.

You have come home.

For Ros

This was going to be
a birthday poem—
it wants to be
a poem
about life.
How
it's always Sunday
sorting the week's
multi-coloured
pills ...
and suddenly
a beloved
grey-haired friend
appears
out of ancient
Kodak memories—
and the day spreads
her arms.

For Judith Mason

The nightingale sang
in the darkness.
The lament of
the mystical nightingale
casting a
spell.
Now
in this silence
my soul
weeps for you.

For Rhona

1.
Late summer.
The ocean is tired,
listless waves
drain
the sleeping sands.
You
are a tired ocean,
life rises
and falls
in the sleepy troughs
of your dreams.

2.
Tonight
the sea is still—
A dark lake
asleep.
You
have returned
to the calm
of your own bed.
The moonpath knows you—
the ocean sings to you.
The candles burning
in your soul's altar
fill all our lives
with light.

3.
Freed
from that ocean
of pain—

Rhona
is finally at rest.
Jacaranda trees
caress her.
In spring
lilac scents
will bathe her.
The white marble
will dance
in the summer's heat.

Oriole

The lonely lament
of the golden oriole.
A single
fragile
limpid call
falling.
I think of Keats.
On that
final
"shore of the wide world"
the oriole
is crying.

Anniversary Poems

1.
On your birthday
I remember the light in Paris—
the way the rooftops danced—
the stinging sun
splintering shadows on café tables—
the yellowing light
quilting our room-size bed
in a small hotel.
We made love
as we always do
celebrating
the light,
the quaint hotel,
being alive—
celebrating
an enchanted world,
the magic of days—
celebrating
that we were well,
that we were
and always would be
in love
as we are now
at this moment
on your birthday.

2.
For
seventeen million
eight hundred and seventy thousand
and four hundred
seconds

I have watched you
asleep
and awake
awed by your beauty
and the serenity
of your soul.
If these were miles
instead of seconds,
I could have circled
the moon
a dozen times.
Perhaps I have...

3.
Thirty-four years—
Time
to count the gains
and the losses.
The hopes and the fears.
Place the tears—
the angry tears—
the overwhelming tears
of loss—
on one enormous pan
of life's gigantic scale.
On the other pan
all the moments
of ecstasy—
the joy
of being alive
authentic
and magically
creative.
Look at the scale
and know
how blessed we are.

4.
I recently read
that Argentinian miners
prefer a lamp
on their chests
to their heads.
It's the heart
that turns the body ...
I thought of us
slowly digging
in this gold mine
we call life.
Each step of the way
you light up
everyone we meet
and every place we see
with your heart.

5.
I still have that lamp
fixed
to my forehead
illuminating dreams ...
Your
heart's flame
still protects
us both
from total darkness.
Holding hands,
we have
found our own way
to walk
in
and out
of shadows.

6.

So many sacred
moments
beyond the reach
of words.
We still
curl and weave
our bodies
in the soft darkness.
Holding.
The silent
implicit
language
of touch.

The Thompson Gallery, November 2010

Homage to Dan, her son who had passed away

1.
Your painting
frightens me.
You have made the canvas
bleed—
The urgency
even the agonising
pain.
It is the voice of
God,
Awesome
and terrifying—
Burning
in crimson rage.

2.
There are moments
when a sunset
changes
the entire world.
Mystic mountains appear.
Buildings hide
in a soft magenta mist.
In that moment
you are
the gentle path winding
in the mountain core.
There are moments
when love
changes
the entire world ...

3.

An entire symphony
frozen
at a single note.
The violins
as always
holding
the central core—
A lonely cello
caught in a
lifting
sensual cry ...
The canvas holds
its breath.

4.

I watch you set the paints
on their canvas loom—
weaving colours hour by hour
weaving love and life
into the magic fabric.
At one moment
it is Night
seducing
flamboyant Day—
the next moment
I feel the endless tussle
of light and shade—
the struggle
of need and fear.
You let the colours fly
tearing the gentle green
with impatient red.
This is the way
the world begins—
This is also the way
it will end ...

5.
This painting
lets me in.
In the beginning
there was canvas.
"Let there be blue,"
you said.
And there was blue.
The red is cradled
and hushed
floating quietly
in breaths of grey.
I listen
to a muted cry
as I walk
in the soft mauve light.

6.
This painting
has a window
allowing the wind
to shred
the dream-red moment.
In the gentle sweep
of fragmenting light—
in the distant
fold
of fading grey—
I can hear it.
A voice
hidden behind
the torn magenta.
A voice
calling.

7.
In the heart's core
of this canvas chest
a wave of light
a rushing flood
muting
the blood and the pain.
A limpid,
silent,
serene
magenta square
floats in the stillness.

8.
I enter this picture
through a blood-cell
window.
I want the wave of paint
to burst
on my chest—
the sense of relief
lifting
beyond the cry
and the pain.
Dark memories
hide
in the red core.

9.
Breathing in
the colour and spirit
of this last painting
a soft curtain
of silence
fills my soul.
The rage
and even the pain
are mute.
I bow
to the stillness.

10.
It's all there
in the black box
of her soul—
each moment
of her journey
recorded.
The aloneness,
the bewildering
absence
of meaning—
and the rage—
the shattering
burning
rage ...

11.
The rage fragments
melting
in the limpid silence.
Love is revealed.
Only love,
delicate,
disarming,
vulnerable,
all-powerful
love.
I know that words can do this—
The right words
waking
the brooding fever
that it lifts and bursts
the even flow
of thought and dream.
This painting sets a stillness
inside me—
A deep brown silence
that always follows pain.

The Sea

I know this sea—
I know
the turbulence
that begins
at the dark core—
The life-deep
Shadows
that pulse and fret.
But still
the wind
is singing,
and the ocean—
The endless
heaving ocean
listens
with ten thousand ears.

Late Harvest Memories

1.
Late harvest memories
time-drenched and ripe.
An autumnal blaze
alive in the grape's core.
The frozen shadows
of winter
are still hidden
beneath
the ageing fruit.
Every poem
seeped in love.

2.
The grapes are ready
to metamorphose
into
wrinkled
sultanas.
Twigs and leaves
edged
with light,
mountains sharp
against
the dying sky.

3.
Late harvest dreams.
Sun-drenched memories—
Life's fruit
ripened and full.
The anticipation of winter—
Frozen shadows.
Every moment
seeped and distilled ...

Tai Chi

I know how
inextricably
moths
are drawn
to a candle flame.
A gigantic
passion
for tiny souls.
Tai Chi
is my candle.
Each moth
I encounter
on this journey
is my brother.

Survivors

Two serious survivors
defiant and naked.
Proclaiming to the
innocent darkness
that we are
Alive.
Tonight
we watched
Netflix
in the nude.

A biography of sorts

Snow has fallen all night. The streets are frozen silent. The trees and houses smell of snow. The scent of snow sits on the edge of all my dreams. Other memories have to be called. I have to look for them. Memories of summer. Men in vests. The smell of cigar smoke weaving the hot Chicago nights into a montage of warm wooden balconies, children running in the sweating darkness and my mother's voice calling me in.

I have to grasp hold of these memories to squeeze a glimpse of an empty brown dining room, the smell of bread and my mother scrubbing the kitchen table. But without effort—I close my eyes—and know that it is snowing.

My mother is crying. This could be a sign. My room has been cleaned. There are clean sheets on the bed. There is no mistaking the signs. The Doctor is coming. I am given clean pyjamas. Not my own. My father's top half. It smells vaguely of tobacco. I am lost in the white slap of wind and snow.

There is a knock on the door. Dr Steinberg is here. He fills the entire apartment. He is in every room. In every corner. This from my dreams. In my memory he is wearing his heavy grey coat with the fur collar. He doesn't take his coat off. His hair is dark and smoothed back. His narrow clipped moustache neatly hugs his upper lip.

The mysterious black bag is on my bed. Dr Steinberg towers above me. His head touches the ceiling. This is only my memory of him. In my dreams, his hands are warm. He holds my wrist and examines a gold watch at the end of a long chain.

The snow is falling. I am suspended above the bare bed. Dr Steinberg, still wearing his coat in the cold of my empty bedroom, floats with me. His warm hands tap my chest.

"Ah yes," he says and smiles. The words "ah yes" float across the room. My parents pass the words back and forth between them. We spin gently into the drifts of snow.

Dr Steinberg holds me in his arms and we both smile. In my memory he speaks of measles and then goes. I remember soon after, a young man arrived with all the medication. And soon after that the groceries began to arrive.

Looking back, I know the stage was set then. We finally returned to South Africa. I joined the Army and spent two years at sea on the hospital ship *Amra* as a Medical Orderly. I was seventeen years old. I was released from the hospital ship in time to join the 1945 intake for Medical students at Wits University. I qualified in 1951. For the past 70 years Dr Steinberg has always been near. I can hear his voice. He sometimes holds my hand.

There was always poetry. I write to Anne Sexton, the American poet. We become friends. It occurred to both of us that we were writing similar confessional poems on either side of the same counter. I, as the psychiatrist in charge of a psychiatric unit, she, as a patient. She read many of my poems in *From Breakfast to Madness*. She made suggestions. We played with alternate words. The title of the book comes out of one of her poems. That was her idea. Tragically she took her life at about the time the book was launched.

I became the editor of the *African Journal of Sexology* and finally the *South African Journal of Sexology* for fifteen years.

I have an Argentinian father. A deeply reserved inhibited man. My mother was Russian, and a stand-up comedienne. She took over at parties. She spoke for my father. She spoke for all of us.

CPSIA information can be obtained
at www.ICGtesting.com
Printed in the USA
LVHW022033131020
668706LV00001B/503

9 781928 433125